CONTENTS

WRITING AND PRINTING

People have been writing things down for thousands of years. Writing began as a way of keeping records and accounts for trade. Soon it was being used to record laws, historical events, sacred texts and stories. Today, writing and printing are an essential part of our lives and one of our most important forms of communication. Think how many times in a day you write something down or read something printed on paper. We use writing and printing in entertainment and education, and for spreading news and ideas. We also rely on ancient writing for all our information about how people lived in the past.

Writing is all around us! Many different styles of writing and printing are used to do different jobs and to get different messages across.

Graffiti is the name given to writing scrawled across a wall, door or pavement. It is often written with spray paint and expresses people's anger or political views. The first graffiti was found on a wall in the ancient Roman town of Pompeii in Italy.

There are newspaper and magazine stands and shops in every city, town and village. Millions of people read newspapers every day to keep themselves informed about the latest world and local news.

The first free public libraries were opened at the end of the 19th century. Until then, people had to pay to borrow books from private libraries. These were often attached to private homes, monasteries and universities.

The word *calligraphy* comes from two Greek words meaning "beautiful writing". Calligraphy is the art of writing by hand. There are many different styles, mainly used for decoration.

Advertisements and logos use the power of the printed word to sell goods, from soft drinks and washing powder to stereo equipment and cars. Bold, bright designs help attract your attention.

Merry Christmas

Joyeux Noël

Fröhliche Weihnachten

How Writing Began

Before writing began, people had to remember everything they needed to know and pass on news, information and stories by word of mouth. But as trade grew and people's lives became more complicated, it became more difficult to rely on memory alone. Writing began some 5,500 years ago, in Sumer (now Iraq), as a way of keeping records and accounts. The first known examples of Sumerian writing are temple accounts, listing heads of cattle and sacks of grain.

SIGNED AND SEALED

The people of the Indus Valley in India had their own form of writing over 4,000 years ago. Thousands of stone seals, used by merchants to mark their goods, have been found in their ancient cities. Each seal has an animal carving and a short inscription. No-one has yet been able to decipher the inscriptions.

WRITING WITH WEDGES

At first, the Sumerians used pictures of animals, people and objects to stand for words. From this developed a form of writing called cuneiform, or "wedge-shaped". The pictures turned into symbols made up of wedge-shaped strokes. These were carved on to tablets of soft clay with square-ended reeds.

CHINESE CHARACTERS

Writing developed early in China too. About 4,000 years ago, people began to use a system of writing in which symbols, called characters, stood for words and ideas. Modern Chinese is very similar to the ancient language. New characters are being invented all the time to express new ideas or words.

EGYPTIAN HIEROGLYPHICS

About 5,000 years ago, the ancient Egyptians began to use a system of picture writing, called hieroglyphics. Each symbol, or hieroglyph, could represent a whole word or a sound. The Egyptians called their writing the "words of the gods". They believed it had been given to them by Thoth, the god of wisdom.

Hieroglyphs were not for daily use. They were reserved for important official matters and inscriptions on temples and royal tombs.

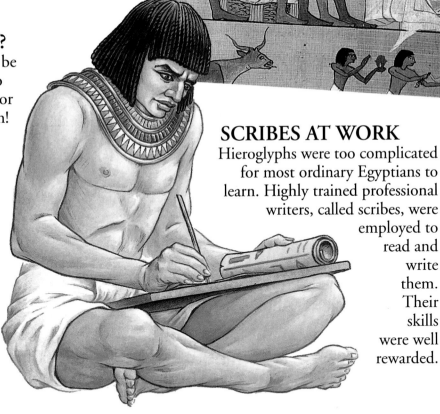

WHICH WAY?

Hieroglyphs could be written from left to right, right to left, or from top to bottom! The pictures themselves provided clues about where to start reading. If a person or animal faced right, you read from right to left. If it faced left, you read from left to right, and so on.

SCRIBES AT WORK

Hieroglyphs were too complicated for most ordinary Egyptians to learn. Highly trained professional writers, called scribes, were employed to read and write them. Their skills were well rewarded.

CRACKING THE CODE

Until 1822, almost 1,500 years after they were last used, no-one knew what the hieroglyphs said. The mystery was solved by a French scholar, Jean-François Champollion. A large, stone slab – the Rosetta Stone – was inscribed with a message to the Egyptian king, written in three scripts – hieroglyphic, demotic (a shorthand form of hieroglyphic) and Greek. By comparing the three, Champollion was finally able to decipher the hieroglyphs.

EARLY ALPHABETS

An alphabet is a system of writing in which letters are used to represent sounds and are joined together to make words. The first alphabet was invented in Syria about 3,600 years ago. Today's alphabets are all descended from it, including the Roman alphabet used to write English and many other European languages.

PHOENICIAN LETTERS

The Phoenicians were sailors and traders who lived in Syria and Lebanon some 3,000 years ago. They helped to spread the idea of an alphabet to the countries around the Mediterranean Sea. Their own alphabet consisted of 22 letters, all of them consonants.

ANCIENT GREEK

The ancient Greeks were among the many peoples who traded with the Phoenicians. They adopted the Phoenician alphabet and adapted it for writing Greek. They added extra letters, includings vowels. They also changed the shape of some of the letters.

ROMAN WRITING

In Italy, the Greek alphabet was adopted first by the Etruscans and then by the Romans. The Romans altered the alphabet for writing Latin, which became the language of their vast empire and the basis of the alphabet we use today to write English. The Roman alphabet had no letters for J, U, W, X and Y. These were added later on.

DID YOU KNOW?
The word *alphabet* comes from the first two letters of the Greek alphabet – alpha and beta.

ALPHABETS AROUND THE WORLD

There are at least 64 different alphabets in use today. Here are examples of letters from some of them:

Greek
ΑΒΓΔΕΖΗΘΙΚΛΜΝΞΟΠΡΣΤΥΦΧΨΩ

Cyrillic
АБВГДЕЖЗИЙКЛМНОПСТУФХЦЧШЩ

Hebrew
א ב ג ד ה ו ז ח ט י כ ל מ נ ס ע פ צ ק ר ש ת ם ן ף ץ

Arabic
جَبَّيِّ ادَّعْرِبْقِ مَوَاهِبِهِ وَأَطَاٰلَ ذَٰلِكَ لُطِفْتَ فِي الأَرْكَانِ عَلَى مَا

Chinese
纟见讠贝车圣乇长门东仑冈戋队

Japanese
ア ヱ イ ヱ ウ ハ ヘ ニ ホ マ カ キ

Devanagari
प्रथमहिं अति अनुराग भवानी ।

WRITING IN RUNES

The Vikings used an alphabet made up of letters called runes. The runes were composed of simple, straight strokes, designed to be carved on to wood or stone. The Vikings believed that the runes had magical qualities and used them to write secret charms and curses.

WRITING SECRET MESSAGES

Try using the runes to write your own secret messages. Write them with a black felt-tip pen so that they stand out. Or you could try carving them on to a piece of polystyrene or a slab of plasticine.

The Viking alphabet was called the futhork, after its first six letters.

WRITE LIKE A ROMAN

In Roman times official documents or announcements were written on papyrus (made of reeds) or carved onto stone. Paper had not been invented. Roman children were only taught to read and write if their parents were rich enough to send them to school. They practised their letters on wooden writing tablets covered with wax. Instead of pens, they wrote with sticks of bronze, bone or ivory, called *styli*. A stylus was sharp at one end for writing and blunt at the other end for smoothing over mistakes. Here you can see how to make your own Roman writing tablet.

A B C D E F G H I K L M
N O P Q R S T V X Y Z

TO MAKE A ROMAN WRITING TABLET

You will need:
- thick cardboard for a base
- strips of wood • glue • rolling pin
- plasticine or modelling clay • knitting needle or empty ballpoint pen • spoon

▲ **2.** Cut four strips of wood. You need two strips 25 cm long and two strips 18 cm long. Glue these on to the baseboard to form a frame.

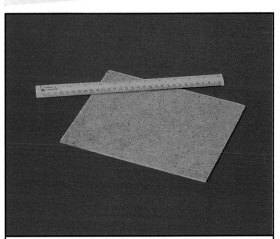

▲ **1.** Cut out a piece of thick cardboard 25 cm x 20 cm to make a baseboard. (You can alter these measurements if you like, to give a larger or smaller rectangle.)

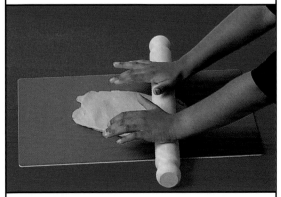

▲ **3.** Roll out the plasticine or modelling clay so that it is roughly the same size as the hole in your frame. Sprinkle some flour on to the plasticine and rolling pin to stop them sticking to each other.

▲ **4.** Lay the plasticine over the frame and gently press it in. Smooth over the surface with the back of a spoon if you leave too many fingerprints!

▲ **5.** Use a knitting needle or a ballpoint pen with the middle taken out to practise your Roman writing. If you make a mistake, smooth it over with the spoon and start again.

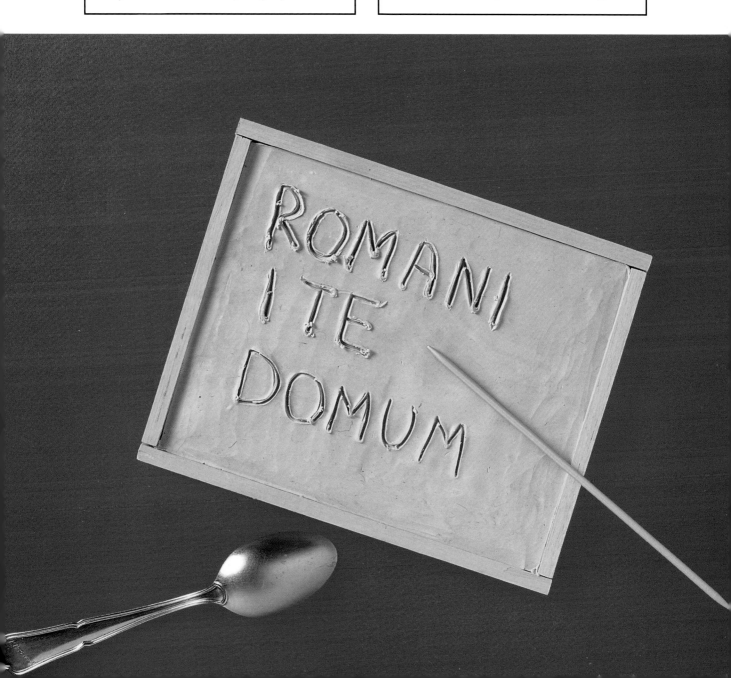

ROMANI
ITE
DOMUM

FROM PAPYRUS TO PAPER

Early writers had no paper to write on. Instead they wrote on pieces of wet clay, wood, bone, bamboo, pottery, silk, wax and palm leaves. Then the ancient Egyptians discovered how to make a type of paper, called papyrus, out of reeds. This was much more practical and much easier to write on.

PAPYRUS PAGES

The ancient Egyptians made papyrus sheets from the stems of the reed-like plants which grew around the River Nile. The stems were cut into thin strips which were overlapped to make sheets. These were then stuck together to form long rolls.

Parchment was usually made from sheepskin, goatskin or calfskin, but the skins of gazelles, antelopes and even ostriches were also used.

PARCHMENT TAKES OVER

Parchment was made from animal skins which had been cleaned, soaked and stretched. They were rubbed with a stone to make them smooth, and then cut into rolls or sheets. As papyrus began to run out, parchment became the most important writing material.

FIRST PAPER

The first real paper was made in China in the 1st century A.D., from rags, water and chips of bark and bamboo. This was mixed into a pulp and spread over a bamboo mat so any excess water could drain off. Then the sheet of wet paper was left to dry before it could be written on. The Chinese kept their paper-making process secret for hundreds of years.

12

PAPER MAKING

Most of today's paper is manufactured in large paper mills. The chips of wood are boiled in water and chemicals to form a soft, mushy pulp. This is washed, bleached and beaten to break up the wood fibres. The pulp then goes into a machine which squeezes excess water from it, dries it and winds it on to giant reels. Until the 19th century, however, paper was made by hand, using frames called moulds.

TO MAKE HANDMADE RECYCLED PAPER

To make the mould:

You will need:
- strips of wood ● screwdriver
- 8 L-shaped braces, with screws
- drawing pins ● masking tape
- piece of old net curtain or fine mesh.

▲ **1.** Have four strips of wood cut to size, two 30 cm long and two 20 cm long. Join them together at the corners with the L-shaped braces to form a rectangular frame.

Stretch the net curtain tightly across one side. Fix in firmly with drawing pins. This is your mould.

▲ **2.** Make a second frame, the same as the first, but slightly bigger (32 cm x 22 cm).

▲ **3.** Place the second frame on the net curtain side of the mould and hold it in place with masking tape.

To make the paper:

You will need:
- 2 plastic buckets or bowls ● water
- small strips of paper ● wooden spoon
- hair dryer (optional)

▲ **1.** Soak the strips of paper overnight in a bucket of water. Drain off any excess water.

▲ **2.** Mash the paper and water into pulp with the wooden spoon.

▲ **3.** Rest the mould on top of the other bucket to catch any drips. Scoop several handfuls of pulp into the mould and spread it out evenly, making sure it reaches right to the edges of the frame. Press it down.

14

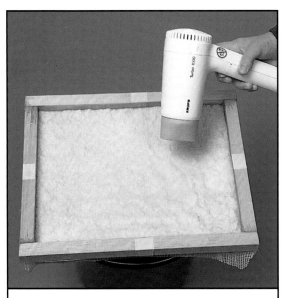

▲ 4. Leave the paper to dry in the mould. This can take quite a long time. Use a hair dryer to dry it faster.

Then gently peel the sheet of paper off the mould.

Because the paper is handmade and has not been bleached or rolled, it will look rougher and darker than the paper you are used to. For lighter paper, use strips of white paper to make your pulp. Press flowers or seeds into the pulp for a special effect.

This marble effect was achieved by dragging a comb through blobs of coloured paint.

15

PEN POWER

Ballpoint pens, fountain pens, felt-tip pens and even pencils are all quite recent inventions. The first writers wrote with reeds, pieces of bone or wood, or brushes. Ink was made from soot mixed with water. The Greeks and Romans used *styli* – narrow sticks of metal, bone or wood. Today, writing has been made much easier by amazing advances in pen technology.

FEATHER PENS

Quill pens were made from goose feathers, cut at one end to form a nib, then dipped in ink. The nib had to be retrimmed regularly with a special knife called a scrivener's knife or a penknife. Quill pens were first used almost 2,500 years ago and were still popular in the 19th century.

FOUNTAIN PENS

In the mid-19th century, Lewis Waterman of the USA made the first successful fountain pen. Metal nibs and fountain pens had already been invented but they either scratched the paper or flooded it with ink. Waterman's pen was the first to write smoothly and cleanly. In the 1950s, the disposable ink cartridge was invented. When it ran out of ink, it could simply be thrown away.

Waterman pens are still made and sold today.

BALLPOINTS

The ballpoint pen, or biro, invented by Lazlo Biró in 1938, is today's most popular writing implement. The pen has a tiny steel ball in its tip. As you write, the ball gets coated with ink from a tube inside the pen and rolls it on to the paper.

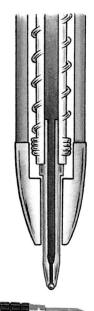

MAKING A QUILL PEN

You can make your own quill pen from a large feather. Practise on a drinking straw first to make sure you get the cuts right. You need to use a sharp knife so ask an adult to help you.

To make a quill pen:

You will need:
- a large, clean feather ● a sharp knife
- a cutting board ● a bottle of ink
- paper

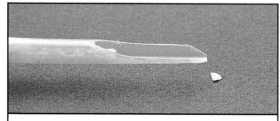

▲ **3.** Now cut a straight line across the tip of the nib.

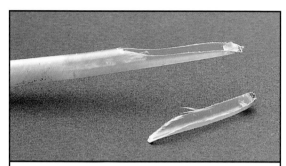

▲ **1.** With an adult's help, cut the end of the feather's shaft at an angle. It is easiest to do this by making a curved cut, starting about 3 cm up from the tip.

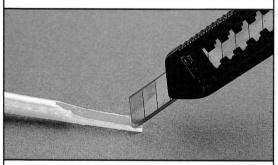

▲ **4.** Make a small slit in the middle of the nib. This will allow the ink to flow more smoothly.

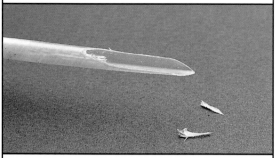

▲ **2.** Cut away the two sides of the tip to form a point. This is the nib. The cuts should curve slightly inwards.

▲ **5.** Dip your quill into the ink, shake off any drips, and start writing! Don't press too hard or you may bend the nib.

BOOKS AND SCROLLS

Until the printing process was invented, books had to be written out by hand, by scribes. This meant that book production was a very time-consuming business and only a small number of books could be made. Despite this, some ancient libraries were enormous. The famous library at Alexandria, Egypt, housed 400,000 books, written on papyrus scrolls.

ROLLS AND SCROLLS

Up to the 4th century A.D., books were written on rolls of papyrus or parchment, called scrolls. In Roman times, scrolls were about 10 metres long. They were stored in leather caskets. In the 4th century A.D., scrolls began to be replaced by the codex, the form of book we have today. This was much easier to read.

Scrolls

Codex

RECTANGULAR BOOKS

In ancient Tibet, books were made from long, narrow palm leaf pages, held together by threads and with carved wooden covers. These books contained the sacred texts of the Buddhist religion of Tibet.

HOLY BOOKS

In Arab countries, scribes wrote out copies of the *Qur'an*, the holy book of Islam. Not a single word could be changed because Muslims (followers of Islam) believe that the *Qur'an* contains the exact words of God. As no pictures were allowed, the scribes tried to make their writing as beautiful and decorative as possible.

The Qur'an

ILLUMINATED MANUSCRIPTS

In the Middle Ages, one of the main reasons for writing was to produce copies of the Bible and other religious works for churches and monasteries. Every monastery had its own *scriptorium*, a room where some of the monks worked as scribes.

The manuscripts were decorated, or illuminated, with pictures and patterns, some drawn using real gold leaf. The capital letters which began a sentence or page were particularly beautiful and ornate.

To illuminate a letter

You will need:
- white cardboard ● tracing paper
- pencil ● fine black felt-tip pen
- selection of coloured felt-tip pens
- gold fineliner pen

1. Choose which letter you would like to illuminate. Sketch it in pencil.

2. Go over the outline with the fine black felt-tip pen.

3. Fill in the colour, using bright colours such as red, blue, green and, of course, gold!

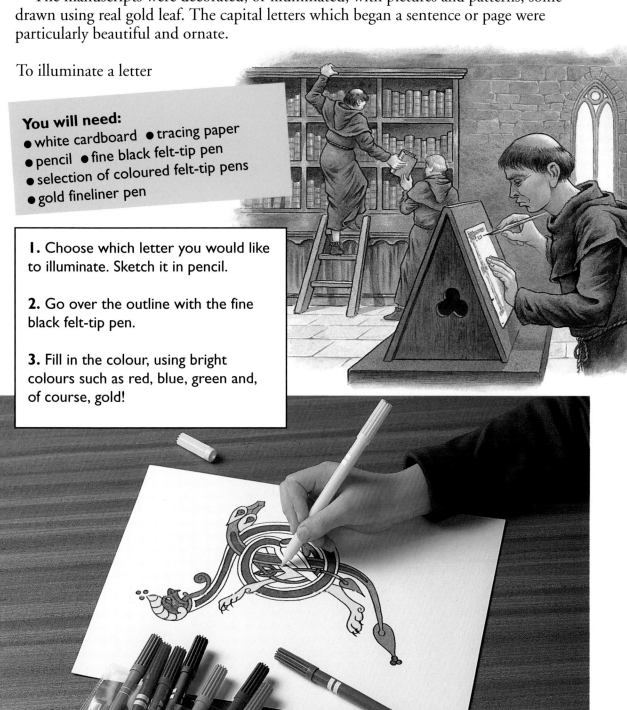

BLOCK PRINTING

Because early books were individually handwritten and illustrated, they took a very long time to produce and were very expensive to buy. As the demand for books grew, a quicker, cheaper way of making them needed to be found. The answer was to print books rather than to write them out by hand.

PRINTING BLOCKS

Over 3,000 years ago, the Chinese used stone seals, with characters carved on them, to stamp official documents. By about 600 A.D. this practice had developed into a type of printing, called block printing. A whole page of text or illustrations could be carved, in reverse and in relief, on a block of wood. This was coated in ink. Then a sheet of paper was pressed over it. The characters were printed on to the paper the right way up.

THE DIAMOND SUTRA

The earliest known printed book was made in China in 868 A.D. It is called the *Diamond Sutra*. The book is in scroll form and contains accounts of the life and teachings of Buddha. It is now in the British Museum in London.

MAKING A BLOCK PRINT

Start by making printing blocks of
individual letters and work up to whole
words. It is probably best to use chunky
letters to begin with as these are easier to
cut or carve out.

TO MAKE A PRINTING BLOCK

You will need:
- small blocks of wood ● glue
- paint or ink ● paintbrush
- craft knife ● thick cardboard
- sheets of paper

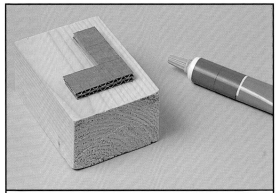

▲ **3.** Stick the card letters together
with some glue. Then glue the
whole letter on to a block of wood.
This is your printing block.

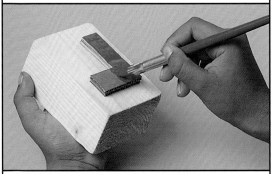

▲ **4.** Paint the letter with some paint
or ink. Then turn it over and press it
on to the paper. The letter should
be printed the right way round.

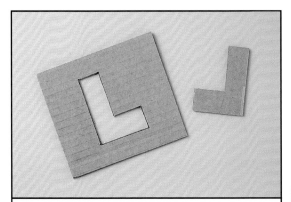

▲ **1.** Decide which letter you would
like to print. Draw the letter on to a
piece of thick cardboard. The letter
should be drawn in reverse on the
cardboard.

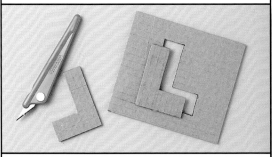

▲ **2.** Cut out the cardboard letter and
use it as a stencil. Now trace and
cut out the letter again.

HOT METAL PRINTING

Even with the block printing technique, books could not be produced quickly or in large quantities and large blocks of text could not be reused. In the 11th century A.D., the Chinese invented "movable type" which was to revolutionise the printing process.

MOVING TYPE

Movable type means that each letter is carved on a block. The blocks are placed next to each other in a frame called a "stick" to make up words. In China, the blocks were made of clay. Later, in Europe, they were made of metal. The great advantage of this process is that the blocks can be used again and again, in any order.

PRINTING PRESS

The first printer to use modern movable type in Europe was the German, Johannes Gutenberg, in about 1436. He invented a wooden printing press based on the presses used to crush grapes for wine making. It pressed paper on to inked type to print each sheet.

The lines of type making up a page were placed in a tray called a "galley". This was coated in ink and paper was pressed on to it.

THE GUTENBERG BIBLE

In 1455, Gutenberg produced the
first printed Bible in the world. It became
known as the "Gutenberg Bible". It is in
two volumes, with 1,200 pages.
Gutenberg printed over 150 copies, a task
which took several years to complete.

WILLIAM CAXTON

The first person to print a book in
English was William Caxton in 1475.
Caxton set up a printing shop in London.
Here he produced a famous edition of
The Canterbury Tales by Geoffrey Chaucer,
which tells the story of a group of pilgrims
on their way to Canterbury. The text was
printed using metal movable type. The
pictures were printed with woodblocks.

The compositor picked out the letters from a
wooden case called a typecase. He set them
in a composing stick, then made the lines up
into a page and locked them in an iron frame,
called a chase, ready to be inked.

A page from The Canterbury
Tales by Geoffrey Chaucer.

TYPESETTING

The letters used in printing are called
type. Arranging the type to form words
and pages is called typesetting. At first
this was done by hand, by compositors.
Using movable type meant any errors
could be corrected.

PRINTING PROGRESS

The printing process invented by Gutenberg hardly changed until the beginning of the 19th century. Then hand presses were gradually replaced by steam-powered presses, which were replaced by rotary presses. These machines helped to speed up the printing process. In the last 50 years, printing has been revolutionised again by the introduction of computer technology. Printing is now faster, cheaper and easier than ever.

ROTARY PRESSES

Today, giant rotary presses are used to print books, newspapers and magazines. At the printer's, the pages of a book, for example, are photographed on to metal sheets called printing plates. These are wrapped around cylinders. Paper is fed through the press to be printed on by the inked plates.

COLOUR PRINTING

To print a colour illustration or photo, it is first scanned by a machine which separates it into four colours and produces a copy in each colour. These are yellow, magenta (red), cyan (blue) and black. Four printing plates are made from these photos. When they are printed on top of each other, they re-combine to produce the original colour of the illustration.

A modern rotary press can print 75,000 copies of a newspaper in an hour.

MODERN TYPESETTING

Until the 1880s, typesetting was done by hand. Then two machines were invented which used keyboards to set type automatically. Another breakthrough came when a machine was invented which set type photographically on paper. This was called photocomposition. Today, most typesetting is done by computer.

WRITING MACHINES

The first modern, manual typewriter was made in the USA in 1874. It was about twice as big as a modern typewriter and very heavy. The typist hit a key which pressed against an inked ribbon and printed the letter on to a piece of paper.

Electric typewriters were invented in the early 20th century, making typing much quicker and easier. Today, word processors are replacing typewriters in most offices. A word processor is like a typewriter with a computer memory.

TYPE AND TYPEFACES

The machine-made letters used for printing are called type. There are many different styles of type, decorative and plain, for different occasions. Each style is called a typeface. Each typeface has a name and particular design features which make it distinctive.

GUTENBERG'S GOTHIC
When Gutenberg began printing, he had to invent his own typeface. He modelled it on a style of handwriting, called Gothic, which was popular in Germany at that time. Some German newspapers continued to be printed in Gothic until quite recently.

abcdefghijklmn

opqrstuvwxyz

ITALIC WRITING
In the 15th century, an Italian printer, Aldus Manutius, began printing books in a new style of type. It became known as Italic because it was devised in Italy. It was based on the handwriting of scribes working in the city of Venice.

abcdefghijklmn

opqrstuvwxyz

This book's main text is set in a typeface called Garamond.

Garamond upper case:
A B C D E F G H I J K L M
N O P Q R S T U V W X Y Z

Garamond lower case:
a b c d e f g h i j k l m n o p
q r s t u v w x y z

The usual, upright style of today's typefaces is called Roman. But some words may be printed in **bold** or in *italic* for emphasis.

USING TYPE

A typeface comes in a range of sizes. These are measured in units called points. A special ruler called a depth scale is used to measure the number of lines of type. To measure this, you also have to take into account the distance between two lines of type.

This text is written in 13/14 point type. This means that the actual type is in 13 point but the distance between each line is 1 point. One line of type has a total depth of 14 points.

To measure a number of lines of 13/14 point type, use the 14 point measure on the depth scale.

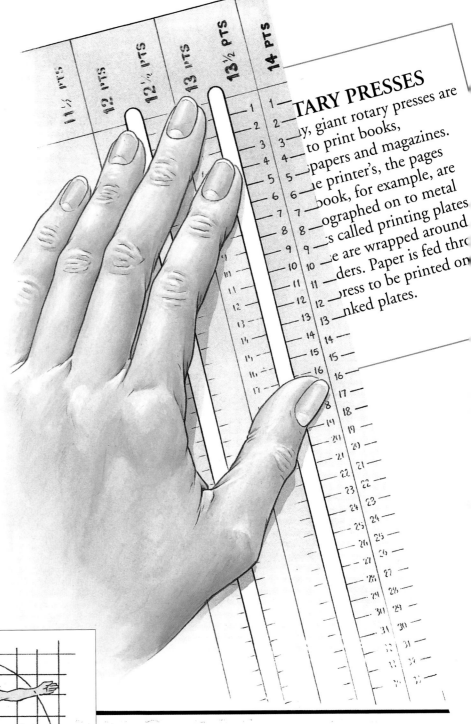

...TARY PRESSES

...y, giant rotary presses are ...to print books, ...papers and magazines. ...e printer's, the pages ...book, for example, are ...ographed on to metal ...s called printing plates ...e are wrapped around ...ders. Paper is fed thro... ...ress to be printed on ...nked plates.

THE HUMAN FACE

Today, there are thousands of typefaces with many more being designed all the time. One of the most dramatic typefaces was designed in the 16th century by a Frenchman, Geoffroy Tory. He used the human body as the framework for his letters.

DESIGN A TYPEFACE

Book, magazine and newspaper designers have to choose the most suitable typeface for the job in hand. A book, for example, needs to be clear and easy to read. An advert in a magazine can use bolder, more artistic type. Here are some tips for designing your own typeface.

YOUR BRIEF

Imagine that you are designing a poster for the school play. You need to give the name of the play and its author, the director's name, the time and location of the performance and the cost of the tickets. This information should be presented clearly but in an eye-catching way. What sort of typeface is most suitable? Big, bold, capital letters would probably work best.

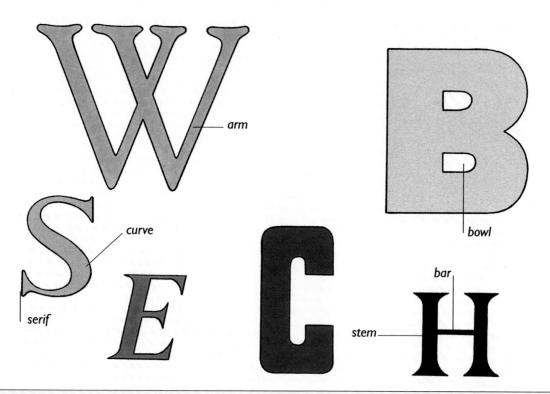

arm

curve

serif

bowl

bar

stem

PARTS OF A LETTER

The different parts of a letter have special names. All the letters in your alphabet should look similar, with the same features and proportions.

Serifs Strokes at the ends of letters. They were first used in Roman times to finish off letters chiselled in stone. A letter without serifs is called sans serif.

Arm A diagonal or horizontal stroke.

Stem A vertical stroke from top to bottom.

Bar A small arm joining two parts of a letter.

Curve A curved part of a letter.

Bowl Area surrounded by a curve.

TO DESIGN A TYPEFACE

You will need:
- squared paper • tracing paper
- plain, white drawing paper • ruler
- pencils • fine black felt-tip pen
- coloured felt-tip pens or marker pens

1. Do some rough sketches of letters first to find the shape and style you want. Try lots of different designs, some with serifs and some without.

2. Draw some horizontal pencil lines to act as guidelines and keep all the letters the same height. It might help to use squared paper to get the proportions of the letters right.

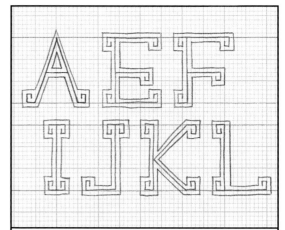

▲ **3.** Now draw the outlines of the letters in pencil between the guidelines. Group similar letters together so that you keep their various parts consistent.

4. When you are happy with the outlines, go over them in black felt-tip. Then fill the letters in with coloured felt-tip or marker pens.

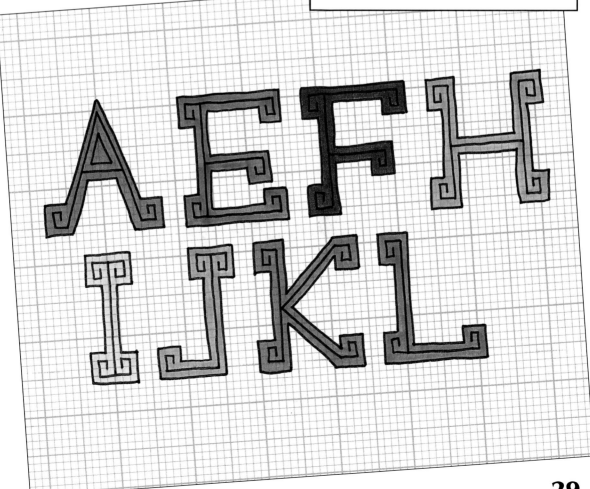

GLOSSARY

alphabet – a system of writing in which letters are used to represent sounds. The letters are joined together to form whole words.

calligraphy – the art of writing by hand. The name comes from two Greek words meaning "beautiful writing."

character – a symbol used to represent a word or an idea. The Chinese language is written in characters.

codex – a book in the form we know today, made of pages bound between two covers. Before the codex, books were made in scroll form.

graffiti – writing or drawings scrawled on a wall.

hieroglyphics – the system of picture writing invented by the ancient Egyptians about 5,000 years ago.

illuminated – a beautifully decorated manuscript.

logo – short for logogram, a character or sign used to represent a word or a name in a short, snappy way.

movable type – each letter is carved onto a metal block. The blocks can be used again and again, in any order.

papyrus – material made of reeds on which people wrote before they discovered how to make paper.

parchment – a material made of animal skin on which people wrote before they discovered how to make paper.

quill – a pen made from a feather (usually goose) and dipped in ink.

runes – the letters of the Viking alphabet. They are composed of clear, straight lines to make them easier to carve into wood or stone.

scribe – a professional writer.

stylus – a stick of metal, bone or ivory, used as a type of pen.

type – the letters used in the printing process.

typeface – a style of type. Some typefaces are very ornate; others are very plain.

typesetting – arranging type into words, sentences and pages, ready for printing.

RESOURCES

BOOKS TO READ

Writing – the Story of Alphabets and Scripts by Georges Jean. Thames and Hudson – *New Horizons* series.

Eyewitness Writing by Karen Brookfield. Dorling Kindersley.

Factfinder Writing & Printing by S & P Harrison (BBC Books).

Lettering and Typography by Tony Potter. Usborne.

Start Exploring – Books by Alison Boyle. Watts Books.

How It's Made – Books by Ruth Thomson. Watts Books.

Making a Book by Ruth Thomson. Watts Books.

Fresh Start – Paper Crafts by John Lancaster. Watts Books.

PLACES TO VISIT

Your local library – they may have a special collection of old books.

A local printer's – look in the phone book for the address, and telephone first.

The British Museum
Great Russell Street
London WC1B 3DG
Tel: 0171 636 1555

The British Library
Great Russell Street
London WC1B 3DG
Tel: 0171 412 7797

PLACES TO WRITE TO

Write to pen and paper manufacturers and other special organisations for information. Always enclose a stamped, self-addressed envelope.

Letters
Hernewood
Gracious Lane
Sevenoaks
Kent TN13 1TJ

INDEX

Additional Photographs:

Ancient Art & Architecture Collection 6; e.t. archive 18, 20 (b); The Fotomas Index 23; Michael Holford Photographs 7; Peter Millard 25; Portfolio Pictures 20 (t); Waterman Pens 16; ZEFA 5, 24.